animals**animals**

Buffalo

by **Phyllis J. Perry**

mc **Marshall Cavendish**
Benchmark
New York

Series consultant
James G. Doherty
General Curator, Bronx Zoo, New York

Marshall Cavendish Benchmark
99 White Plains Road
Tarrytown, NY 10591-9001
www.marshallcavendish.us

Library of Congress Cataloging-in-Publication Data

Perry, Phyllis Jean.
Buffalo / by Phyllis J. Perry.
p. cm. — (Animals, animals)
Summary: "Describes the physical characteristics, behavior, and habitat of
buffalo"—Provided by publisher.
Includes bibliographical references and index.
ISBN 0-7614-1866-0
1. American bison—Juvenile literature. I. Title. II. Series.

QL737.U53P388 2005
599.64'3—dc22
2004021438

Photo research by Joan Meisel

Cover photo: Michael S. Bisceglie/Animals Animals

The photographs in this book are used by permission and through the courtesy of: *Animals Animals:* 7, Manoj Shah; 14,
32-33, 38, Richard Kettlewell; 16, Darren Bennett; 18, McDonald Wildlife Photography; 28, Michael S. Bisceglie; 31,
Donna Ikenberry. *Bruce Coleman, Inc.:* 1, 9, 15, Erwin & Peggy Bauer; 4, John Hyde; 6, Brian Miller; 8, Jonathan T.
Wright. *Corbis:* 10, Layne Kennedy; 20, Francis G. Mayer; 23, Paul A. Souders; 25, Bettmann; 41, Jan Butchofsky Houser.
North Wind Picture Archives: 26. *Peter Arnold, Inc.:* 17 (bottom), Fred Bruemmer; 24, KLEIN; 30, James L. Amos; 34,
Alan & Sandy Carey; 35 (top), Peter Weimann; 35 (bottom), Kevin Schafer; 36, William Campbell; 43, Peter Frischmuth.
Photo Researchers, Inc.: 17 (top), Tom & Pat Leeson.

Series redesign by Adam Mietlowski

Printed in China

3 5 6 4 2

Contents

1 The Buffalo

A herd of buffalo quietly grazes in the sunlit morning. But they are not alone. Native American buffalo runners are hidden among the herd, disguised under animal hides. They suddenly leap up shouting. Frightened buffalo scatter, racing toward a cliff. Reaching the edge, the buffalo in the lead cannot stop in time and fall to their death. Others topple over behind them. The hunters quickly move in. They kill their injured *prey* with spears, arrows, and clubs.

Scenes like this were common at places called *buffalo jumps.* In the early nineteenth century, there were about 40 million buffalo roaming the plains of North America. They were found from California to

The buffalo has a short, thick neck topped by a shoulder hump.

Pennsylvania and from Florida to Canada's Great Slave Lake. But their favorite *habitat* was the Great Plains.

Scientists think buffalo first came to North America from Asia. They crossed over a piece of land that once connected the two continents near what is today called the Bering Strait. They thrived in their new home.

The buffalo's massive head helps make it North America's largest land animal.

Buffalo, like cows, belong to a group of mammals called *bovids*. Bovids are covered with fur, have horns and hooves, and nurse their young with milk. In addition to buffalo and cows, other animals among the bovid *species* include yaks, bighorn sheep, cape buffalo, and water buffalo.

The cape buffalo is found in most of southern and central Africa.

A buffalo is covered with long woolly hair that is usually dark brown.

Buffalo graze mostly in the morning and evening.

The buffalo has more than one name. To some, it is the North American bison. The Lakota Sioux called this great beast *Tatanka*, which means "spirit." They named it out of respect for an animal they relied on not only for their food but for their clothing and shelter as well.

Relatives of the buffalo once lived in western Europe until the eleventh century. Called *wisents*, these European buffalo were forest animals that ate leaves, ferns, and bark. Some have been reintroduced to the wild. A few wisents can be seen today in zoos and on animal preserves in Poland and Russia.

2 What Are Buffalo?

Buffalo are among the largest land animals living today in the United States and Canada. Covered with shaggy brown fur, a male buffalo stands about 6.5 feet (about 2 meters) tall. A male, called a *bull*, may weigh up to 2,400 pounds (1,089 kilograms). Extremely large bulls may reach 3,000 pounds (1,361 kilograms). Female buffalos, called *cows*, are somewhat smaller than the males.

There are two groups that make up North America's buffalo species: wood buffalo and plains buffalo. The wood buffalo is larger and darker in color than the plains buffalo. Its fur is woolier, and it has a squarish hump on its back. Wood buffalo are

Long hairs on the chin of a buffalo form a beard.

The Buffalo:

A closer look at a buffalo skeleton. It helps to support . . .

Inside and Out

. . . the body of this large land mammal.

Early explorers were facinated by the buffalo's unusual look.

mainly found in northern Canada—in Alberta, British Columbia, Saskatchewan, and the Northwest Territories. Sure-footed wood buffalo have been seen climbing high up the sides of mountains.

Plains buffalo live on the grasslands of the United States and Canada. The humps on their backs are more rounded than those of wood buffalo.

Buffalo are like several animals in one. They have manes like a lion, horns like a cow, beards like a goat, and humps like a camel. They have

14

large heads, short necks, sharp horns, and small tufted tails. For such a large animal, the buffalo can run quickly, reaching speeds of up to 35 miles (56 kilometers) an hour.

Buffalo make a variety of noises, including grunts, snorts, and squeaks, which they use in different situations. During mating season, a bull may paw at the ground, stare, snort, and swing his horns to frighten away another bull. At other times, a buffalo may make a loud bellow. When it bellows, the buffalo's mouth hangs open and its tongue dangles down. Some bellows can be heard for a distance of 3 miles (4.8 kilometers).

Herds of buffalo once roamed the Great Plains of the United States and Canada. Now they are only found in parks and preserves.

Species Chart

Height: 5 to 6.5 feet (1.5 to 2 meters)
Length: 84 to 144 inches (2.1 to 3.7 meters)
Weight: 700 to 3,000 pounds (318 to 1,361 kilograms)
Life Span: 15 to 25 years

Like its relatives, a plains buffalo usually drinks at
a watering hole or stream once a day.

Wood buffalo are generally taller and less stocky than plains buffalo.

This European bison, or wisent, rests in a forest in Poland.

In winter, buffalo brush away snow with their beards and paw through the icy crust to find shrubs and plants below.

18

A buffalo's life varies with the seasons. Even in their warm woolly coats, winter is a hard time. To find food, buffalo sweep their beards back and forth on the ground to brush away the snow. They burrow into deep snow, pushing with their noses and swinging their great heads, hunting for grass.

In spring, buffalo rub against rocks, trees, and fence posts to shed their shaggy winter coats. Often they will return several times to the same rocks, called rubbing stones, to groom their fur and skin.

Buffalo also like to roll and wallow on the ground. This helps to remove shedding hair and relieves insect bites. When large groups of buffalo roll and thrash about, they create *wallows*. Many of the wallows fill with rain and form small temporary pools of water. Sometimes early westward settlers who followed buffalo trails watered their stock in these prairie ponds.

3 A Native Species

For thousands of years, buffalo provided food, clothing, and shelter for the Native Americans who lived on the plains. Among these Native American groups were the Arapaho, Blackfoot Confederacy, Cheyenne, Comanche, Crow, Kiowa Apache, and Pawnee.

The Native Americans told stories and performed ceremonies involving the buffalo. The Blackfeet prepared themselves for the Sun Dance by going into a sweat lodge made of buffalo skin stretched over willow branches. Rocks were heated outside and then brought into the lodge. They were then sprinkled with water from a buffalo horn to create steam, which cleansed the men's bodies. A painted buffalo skull was

After horses were introduced in North America, Native Americans hunted buffalo from horseback.

placed on top of or near the lodge. Hanging down in the center of the lodge was a buffalo tail. The warriors stood inside the lodge and talked of their brave deeds. For each deed, they placed a stick on the fire in the center of the lodge. The greatest warrior was the one who placed enough sticks on the fire to scorch the buffalo tail.

Head-Smashed-In Buffalo Jump in Alberta, Canada, was a popular hunting spot 5,700 years ago when it was common for groups of Native Americans to hunt on foot and drive buffalo over cliffs. But hunting changed in the 1500s after the Spanish brought horses to North America. Native Americans became skilled riders and used their horses in great buffalo hunts. They were armed with arrows, or sometimes guns, to kill buffalo.

After a buffalo hunt, there was much work to be done. Meat was boiled, roasted, and dried. Some of it was then pounded and mixed with melted buffalo fat and dried berries to form pemmican. Pemmican wrapped in rawhide sacks would last a long time without spoiling.

Buffalo were more than just a source of food, though. The flesh and sometimes the hair on the

Native American hunters often drove frightened buffalo off a cliff such as this one, Head-Smashed-In Buffalo Jump, at Fort Macleod, in Alberta, Canada.

Horns, found on both male and female buffalo, curve upward and slightly forward.

buffalo hides were scraped off. The hides were dried in the sun. Stiff pieces of hide were used to make boats, drums, and rattles. Softer pieces were needed for clothing such as skirts, shirts, pants, shoes, and bags. The hides were also used to make tepee covers and blankets. Hides were softened in different ways. The Blackfeet used a mixture of buffalo fat, brains, and liver, which they rubbed and worked into the hides.

These two Native Americans scrape a buffalo hide, a step in making leather.

Other parts of buffalo were also used. Hooves might be used for rattles, and horns were made into children's tops. Buffalo hair was braided and twisted into ropes, belts, and handles. Bones were turned into war clubs, peace pipes, whistles, scrapers, and other tools. The teeth of buffalo were strung into necklaces. Sinew, which is the tissue that connects muscles to bones, was used as thread for sewing. Skulls might be made into headdresses.

Did You Know . . .

Wherever skinners had worked on buffalo hides, they left behind huge piles of bones. These buffalo bones were gathered up and hauled away by wagons and trains to be used to make fertilizer and bone china and to refine sugar.

Once railway lines reached the prairie, white hunters would often shoot buffalo for sport from inside the train.

Did You Know . . .

Originally a buffalo hunter, William Cody, also known as Buffalo Bill, organized his Wild West Show in 1883. The audience watched him shoot blank bullets and *stampede* the buffalo out of the show area.

When Europeans moved to North America, they began to hunt buffalo too. In the 1800s many settlers hunted on horseback, using guns to kill the buffalo on the Great Plains. When the railroads were being built, the work crews lived mostly on buffalo meat. Once trains were running, special trips for hunting buffalo were offered. Passengers opened the train windows and shot at the buffalo herds.

Buffalo hides were used by people across America for winter coats, overshoes, blankets, and sleigh robes. Hunters and skinners teamed up to still hunt, or shoot from one spot. Hunters would get as close as possible to the buffalo and then open fire. A good hunter could kill around one hundred buffalo per day, and skinners would remove the hides. In the process, the buffalo population was almost destroyed. Luckily, today it has made a comeback.

4 The Herd

Today most buffalo live in small herds. About twenty females will join together. The males form a different group. When it is time to mate, in August and September, the groups of cows and bulls come together. Between 270 and 285 days later, in May or June, buffalo cows go off alone to have their babies.

The cow and newborn calf rejoin the herd after three or four days. Although most calves are reddish brown, a rare white buffalo is sometimes born. Native Americans considered a white buffalo to be a sacred animal with special powers.

Buffalo calves begin to get small bumps on their heads when they are about six or seven weeks old.

For safety, calves stay close to their mothers.

This buffalo and her nursing calf live near Gillette, Wyoming.

Their horns grow from these bumps. When they are a couple of months old, they start to develop humps on their backs. The nursing calves stay close to their mothers for a year. When the calves are old enough, they begin to graze and drink water, even though they may still be nursing.

A predator wanting to harm a young buffalo would have to deal with its watchful mother first.

As they grow, the calves continue to change. Their *tawny* coats turn to a dark brown. As winter approaches, calves grow thick coats, like all buffalo, to protect them against the cold. Calves stay with the herd of cows until they are two or three years old. Then the young females remain with the cows, and the males leave to join the other bulls. In the wild, buffalo live to be about twenty.

After a day of running and playing, these calves share a quiet moment.

Even a powerful grizzly bear hesitates to take on a full-grown buffalo.

Living in a herd helps to keep buffalo safe from *predators.* Buffalo rely on keen smell and hearing to help protect them from attack. Among their predators are grizzly and black bears, packs of gray wolves, and cougars, which frequently seek out the young, old, or sick buffalo as their prey.

A pack of gray wolves might occasionally kill an old, sick, or very young buffalo.

A cougar usually eats deer, but it will eat other animals including buffalo.

Cowbirds may perch on or near buffalo in order to eat the insects that the buffalo attract. These birds rest on the back of a buffalo in Yellowstone National Park.

Led by one of the oldest cows, the buffalo move about during the year to different areas. Buffalo eat grass and other ground cover. They follow the same well-worn paths each year looking for food.

Did You Know . . .

Birds often gather near herds of buffalo. Cowbirds perch on the backs of buffalo and eat the insects that live in the buffalos' fur. This *symbiotic relationship* helps the buffalo get rid of pests and provides food for the birds.

5 Saving the Buffalo

At the beginning of the nineteenth century, about 40 million buffalo roamed the North American continent. By the end of the century, fewer than one thousand were left. In 1894, just in time to save the remaining buffalo, the United States government passed a law to fine or jail those who hunted the few that were left in Yellowstone National Park in Wyoming. That same year, Canada passed a law also protecting buffalo. Slowly the small herds of buffalo in the United States and Canada began to increase in size.

In 1905 the American Bison Society was formed at the Bronx Zoo in New York City. The zoo began

Buffalo are usually calm and peaceful, but they sometimes fight for rank in the herd and may charge if cornered.

collecting the few bison that had survived because they were owned privately and began to breed the animals and build up its herd. Later, groups of buffalo born at the zoo were sent to Oklahoma and South Dakota and released into the wild. Today the large herds found in those areas are descendants of animals from the Bronx Zoo.

Another place where buffalo herds are increasing is on Native American reservations. The Crow's wild herd was begun in the 1930s. The original animals came from Yellowstone, Montana's National Bison Range, and from some private ranches as well.

Today buffalo continue to grow in number. Protected herds live in Yellowstone National Park, Canada's Banff National Park, the Wichita Mountains Wildlife Refuge in Oklahoma, Theodore Roosevelt National Park in North Dakota, the Montana National Bison Range, and in Alberta's Wood Buffalo National Park. In Custer State Park in South Dakota there is a herd of about one thousand buffalo. The largest herd of wood buffalo in Canada consists of more than two

Did You Know . . .

The buffalo once appeared on the ten-dollar bill starting in 1901. People referred to this as the Buffalo Bill. The buffalo also appeared on nickels beginning in 1913.

thousand animals in the Mackenzie Bison Sanctuary near Fort Providence, Northwest Territories. Some ranchers raise their own herds of buffalo and sell them for their meat.

Highly prized, white buffalo fur is used in the White Buffalo Dance headdress.

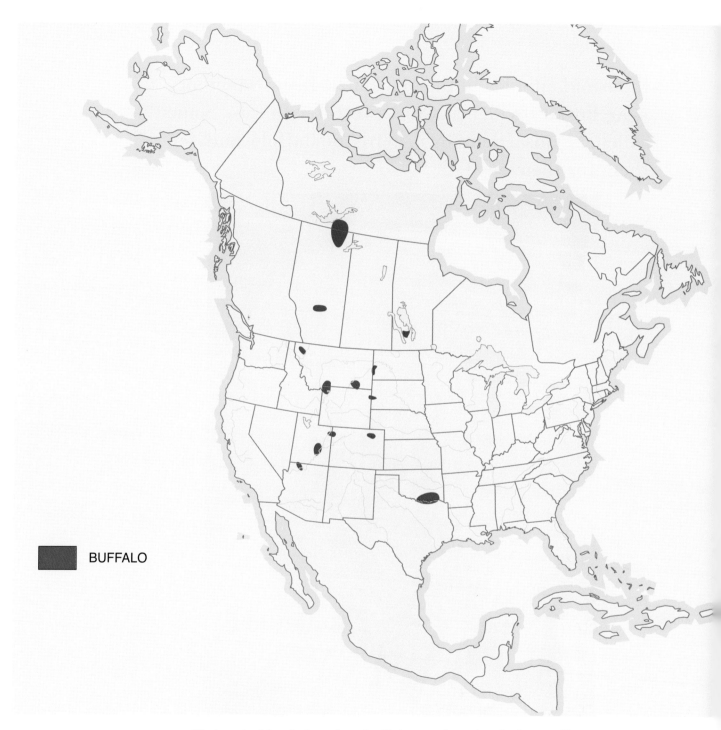

BUFFALO

Today, in North America, buffalo are found only in small groups.

This large herd of buffalo is being rounded up at Custer State Park in South Dakota.

People have learned lessons from the past. They saw the great wild herds of buffalo that numbered in the millions destroyed by over-hunting. Concern led to action. Laws were passed, and the endangered buffalo was protected. This magnificent animal, once the symbol of the plains, has survived. Nearly a quarter of a million buffalo live in North America today on public and private land. The buffalo is thriving once again.

During the third week in August, the Crow Nation holds the Crow Fair to celebrate buffalo days. People from all over the reservation gather at a certain spot and put up their tepees. The pow-wow, as this gathering is called, lasts for several days. The Crow hold dance contests, drumming contests, horse races, and rodeo competitions.

Glossary

bovid: A kind of mammal, with horns and hooves, that eats only plants.

buffalo jump: A natural feature, such as a cliff, where Native Americans stampeded buffalo, making them jump to their deaths.

bull: The adult male of several kinds of animals, including the buffalo.

cow: The adult female of several kinds of animals, including the buffalo.

habitat: The place where an animal lives.

predator: An animal that hunts and kills other animals for food.

prey: Animals that are hunted and eaten by predators.

species: An animal that is different from other animal types and breeds only with its own kind.

stampede: A large group of frightened animals that are running away.

symbiotic relationship: A close association of two separate species that benefits both.

tawny: Having an orange-brown color.

wallow: A place where an animal comes to roll on the ground.

wisent: A relative of the buffalo that once roamed western Europe.

Find Out More

Books

Becler. John E. *The North American Bison.* San Diego: KidHaven Press, 2003.

Brodsky, Beverly. *Buffalo: With Selections from Native American Song-Poems.* New York: Marshall Cavendish, 2003.

Hoyt-Goldsmith, Diane. *Buffalo Days.* New York: Holiday House, 1997.

Johnston, Marianne. *Buffaloes.* New York: PowerKids Press, 1997.

Midge, Tiffany. *Animal Lore and Legend—Buffalo.* New York: Scholastic, 1995.

Potts, Steve. *The American Bison.* Mankato, MN: Capstone Press, 1997.

Robbins, Ken. *Thunder on the Plains: The Story of the American Buffalo.* New York: Atheneum Books for Young Readers, 2001.

Stone, Lynn M. *Bison Farms.* Vero Beach, FL: Rourke, 1999.

Wilkinson, Todd. *Bison: Bison Magic for Kids.* Milwaukee: Gareth Stevens, 1995.

Wrobel, Scott. *Bison.* Mankato, MN: Smart Apple Media, 2001.

Web Sites

http://www.worldalmanacforkids.cm/explore/animals/buffalo.html
Provides interesting facts about the water buffalo and cape buffalo.

http://montanakids.com/dbengine/subcat.asp?Subcat=Jumping+Buffalo
Discusses places where buffalo were driven off cliffs during hunts.

http://www.kids.net.au
On this site for Kids & Teens School Time Science, you can read an informative article about North American buffalo.

About the Author

Phyllis Perry and her husband, David, live in Boulder, Colorado. From Boulder, it is only a day's drive to Custer State Park in South Dakota, where they often go to photograph and enjoy the buffalo that live there. Phyllis Perry is the author of more than forty books for children and educators including many nonfiction books about animals and three Fribble Mouse Library Mysteries, *Mr. Crumb's Secret*, *The Secret of the Silver Key*, and *The Secrets of the Rock*.

Index

Page numbers for illustrations are in **boldface**.